The Diver

Written by Anne Curtis

Illustrated by Chris Corner

Collins

The *Treasure Seeker* weighs its anchor. If all goes well,
they'll return with the legendary figurehead
of a mermaid of pure, painted gold.

The captain leans over to study the chart.
He imagines the ancient ship lying somewhere
out there, on the sea bed.

On the prow of the ship the diver sits alone.

The captain is a man who prides himself on knowing his crew, but the diver keeps himself to himself. All they know is that he's the best, probably in the world!

Looking into the waves, the diver remembers how, as a child,
he learnt to dive for pearls.

4

He thinks of his small village at the edge of the ocean.
The sea was his playground. He could hold his breath
for longer and go deeper than anyone in his village.

The sun slowly sets over a calm sea. Seagulls dip and dive in the wake of the *Treasure Seeker* as she chugs along.

The hours pass. The captain looks across at the diver and calls out, "We must be close by now?"

The diver is aware of his reputation and his ability
to find treasure. "Trust me. I know the sea."

A full moon lights up the black water.
At last the diver speaks, "Here! Stop here!"

The engines are stopped and they drop the anchor.
"Time you were on your way, then!"

The diver gives a mock salute.

9

He returns to the deck in a suit of thick cloth that joins his metal helmet in a ring of nuts and bolts.

He peers through a circle of glass and lifts one heavy boot ... then the other ... clunk-clunk! He can hear the sound of his own breathing drifting through the air pipe.

10

The diver nods, "Ready."

They lower him over the side of the ship.
He sinks into the soft surface of the ocean.
His lead boots pull him down. His lifeline
trails behind him.

The men lean out over the side of the ship and watch as the diver sinks deeper and deeper.

Silver fish circle his head, making
a crown of sparkling diamonds.

13

The crew lower a line to him.
He tugs twice, "All's well."

Ahead of him, he glimpses the golden figurehead
with its beautiful, painted face.

He wastes no time and wraps the line tightly around
the golden fishtail. He tugs three times. "Pull!"

The diver watches the figurehead slowly
rise from the deep. His job is done.

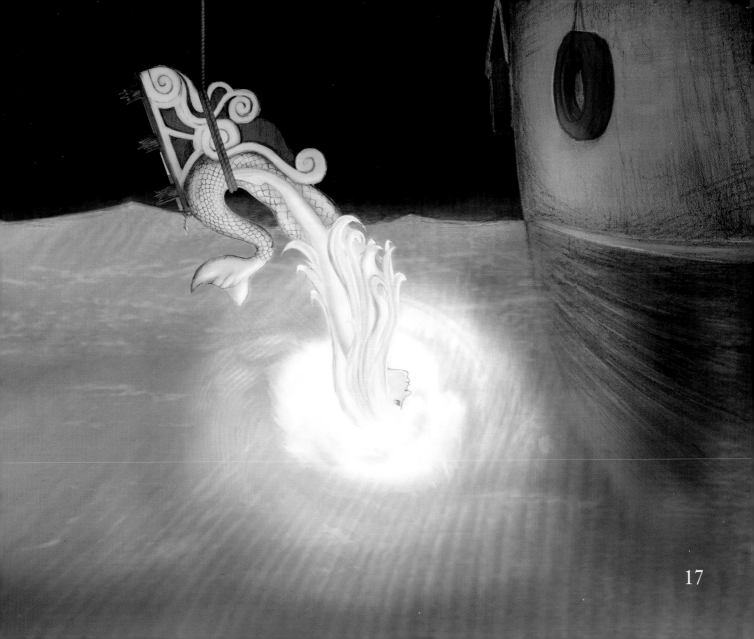

He casts off his diving suit as if shedding his skin
and watches it fall to the sea floor. His air pipe
floats to the surface as he swims off in silence,
following the silver fish.

18

He knows that soon he must return to the world above.
The crew are already searching for him.

But this is the diver who can hold his breath longer than anyone.
Time enough to search for the real treasures of the sea.

21

The best diver

23

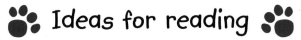 Ideas for reading

Written by Gillian Howell
Primary Literacy Consultant

Learning objectives: *(reading objectives correspond with Turquoise band; all other objectives correspond with Sapphire band)* read independently and with increasing fluency longer and less familiar texts; know how to tackle unfamiliar words that are not completely decodable; compare the usefulness of techniques such as visualisation, prediction and empathy in exploring the meaning of texts

Curriculum links: History, Citizenship

Interest words: treasure, weighs, anchor, legendary, ancient, ocean, calm, reputation, salute

Resources: pens, paper

Word count: 482

Getting started

- Read the title together and look at the cover illustration. Ask the children to suggest what this book will be about and if they know anything about diving already. Discuss the outfit on the cover and what it might be like to wear.

- Ask the children to read the back cover blurb. Ask them if this gives a clue about the content. Can they predict what treasures the diver might find?

Reading and responding

- Ask the children to read the story quietly. Listen in as they read and remind them to use their knowledge of phonics and contextual clues to work out new words. Support them as necessary, e.g. on p2 prompt the children to use the hard *c* in *anchor*.

- As the children read, pause occasionally and ask them about the character of the diver, e.g. on p7, ask why the diver says "Trust me. I know the sea."

- Ask the children to read to the end of the book. Praise them for reading with expression and support children who need extra help.

Returning to the book

- Ask the children to give a personal response to the story and the character of the diver. Ask them to think of words that could describe him, e.g. mysterious, aloof, secretive.